The Challenge

The Challenge

Brenda and Richard Ward

TATE PUBLISHING
AND ENTERPRISES, LLC

Published by Tate Publishing & Enterprises, LLC
127 E. Trade Center Terrace | Mustang, Oklahoma 73064 USA
1.888.361.9473 | www.tatepublishing.com

Tate Publishing is committed to excellence in the publishing industry. The company reflects the philosophy established by the founders, based on Psalm 68:11,

"The Lord gave the word and great was the company of those who published it."

Book design copyright © 2015 by Tate Publishing, LLC. All rights reserved.
Cover design by Gian Philipp Rufin
Interior design by Manolito Bastasa

Published in the United States of America

ISBN: 978-1-68028-567-3
Religion / Christian Life / Devotional
14.12.03

—◠◡◠—

Heavenly Father, we thank you for your Holy Spirit and
for your guidance throughout this book.
May it bring honor and glory to your Holy name and may
we all be found
doing your work when you call us home.
We love you and praise you, Lord!

—◠◡◠—

This book is in honor of Reverend Tollie Bonds, an ordained minister with the Assembly of God Church until her home going in 1983. Thank you for all the days you spent with me as a child showing me firsthand what a life of service to God was like. You are the only person I have ever known to have calloused knees from praying. I can still hear your voice echoing through the Sunday school rooms as you called each of our names before God. You left a wonderful legacy as a pastor, founder of churches, soul winner, friend, wife, mom, and grandmother, but most importantly, the legacy of a Godly woman in love with her savior!

You set the bar high for your family to follow, and for that we are all thankful!

My hope is that *The Challenge* makes you smile.

I love and miss you, Grandma!

ACKNOWLEDGMENTS

Thank you to…

Our children, who are truly blessings from God. Kristen, Erin, Beth, Ben, and Hope, we love you!

Our parents, Otis and Vera Ward and Earnest and Caretta Smith. Thank you for raising us to love the Lord!

Our family, pastors, friends, volunteers, for your example in serving God.

Special thanks to you, the reader, for taking *The Challenge*. Changing this world for better starts with each of us! God bless you!

CONTENTS

Every morning, we wake up to a whole array of choices. Where will we go? What will we do today? The amazing thing that happens to most of us is that time gets totally away from us, never again to be regained…moments, minutes, hours—lost forever!

How many days are we letting slip by us because we are so engrossed in our "lives" that we never even consider other people's problems, hurts, fears, and disappointments? We are too busy working, fishing, talking, Facebooking, texting, studying, eating, cleaning, and dozens of other distractions.

It is amazing that for a rather intelligent society we are totally missing the obvious. We believe there is a God, we profess the Bible as his living word. We know we will live a hundred years on earth, if we are lucky, and then an eternity in heaven or hell, depending on where we have made our reservation. In Revelations 22:12 (KJV), God says, "And behold, I come quickly and my reward is with Me to give everyman according as his work shall be." Let me repeat that, in case anyone wasn't listening closely. God is coming quickly, and he is going to bring his reward for you according to your work for him!

Funny how we let things slip up on us. Retirement, for instance. We all know we are going to retire somewhere around sixty-five years old. Yet most of us never save near enough to fully enjoy retirement. Likewise, we let our life tick by, and never really face the reality of eternity and our heavenly rewards.

The thing about our eternity is that we have no idea what day *our* eternity will begin. Will you cross over to eternity today? Tomorrow? Ten years from now? Or will the Lord sound the trumpet and surprise us all? We have no promise of tomorrow. That statement makes me sad. Not for me. I know that I asked the Savior into my heart years ago, and have served him. But what about the whole world? How many people do you see on fire for God? God said in Revelations 3:15–16, "I know thy works that thou are neither cold nor hot: I would thou wert cold or hot, so then because thou are lukewarm...I will spew thee out of my mouth."

Take a minute to absorb this fact. The estimated population for the world is seven billion people, with only 2.7 billion estimated Christians.

Let's just imagine for a moment that the trumpet is sounding, and Jesus is in the clouds. Just like he said, in an instant, no warning. How many of our friends and family would you say are *hot*, on fire for the Lord? How many are lukewarm or cold? Scary thought, isn't it?

How many will be left behind? How many lost forever? Revelations 20:15 says, "Whosoever was not found written in the book of life was cast into the lake of fire."

Now I have a question for you. Which would be the most important thing I could do—share the love of God, the message of salvation to a sinful world, or watch three hours of TV?

No brainer, right?

We want to present you with a challenge. A challenge that is commissioned by God and has been since the beginning of time. To equip us for this challenge, God gave us a book of instruction—the Bible. And a friend and counselor to lead us along the way—the Holy Spirit. It's time we got serious about it!

We established a nonprofit Christian ministry that feeds and clothes several thousand families. Over time, you become attached to these families and their situations. It has been surprising how many of these friends have died suddenly and never made it back to our ministry. Left this world suddenly, without another chance for us to witness to them. Their time is up. Do you hear me?

Their time on earth is up!

No second chances! No more tomorrows!
Their fate for eternity is set!

Your time is not up!

You have today, but no promise of tomorrow,
but you have *right now*!
With everything that is within us
we scream from these pages
We plead!
We beg!

Get busy! Be about your Heavenly
Father's business!
Your time is going to be up!

You can have millions or billions of dollars.
Expensive houses, fancy cars, and many other
treasures. But if you have not worked for the Lord,
where is your eternal reward?

PLEASE

PLEASE

PLEASE

GET BUSY!

But first things first!

First of all, if you have not made Jesus your Lord and Savior, now is the time. *This* is the day. Do not wait! You have no promise of the rest of this day.
You do not have to be perfect to come to the Lord, He loves you so much he died for you!
If you want to start the best life you can possibly have. Start a new life with Jesus today, it's simple.

Say this prayer, with your heart.

Heavenly Father, I know that I am a sinner in need of a Savior. Jesus, I know that you died on the cross so that my sins can be forgiven. I believe that on the third day you rose from the grave, and through your sacrifice, I can have eternal life. I ask you to forgive me, and wash my sins away. From this day on, I am a new creature in you, a child of the King. I will serve you with all that is within me. I know my sins are now forgiven, and I know my name is now written in the book of Life.

It is important to let someone know of your decision to live for God. Be sure and share with a friend. And we would love to know too so that we can keep you in our prayers. Please e-mail us at TheFathersStore@aol.com and let us know of your good news!

Get into God's word, it is his instructions! It will guide you! It will be your defense when the enemy comes against you. It will encourage you. It will feed your faith and fuel your spiritual growth.

Also, it is important that you get in a good Bible-based church. You will enjoy being with people who are on the same path as you. And it certainly is encouraging and uplifting to be in God's house. You will get recharged each week.

You do not have all the answers, nor do you have to. You may be feeling empty or lonely. You may be in bondage because of addictions. Whatever it is, God is more than able to help. After all, do you really think that any of your issues are too much for the God who created the universe?

You will not be perfect. None of us are. When you mess up, ask the Lord to forgive you, dust yourself off, and do better day by day. Satan will throw everything at you to get you to stumble. Then he will try to convince you that your salvation is not real and that you are not worthy. But God loves you! He loves you so much that he sent his only Son, Jesus, to die for you. And the amazing story of his grace is that even if you were the only person on the earth, he still would have sent Jesus—just for you. Unworthy? Not hardly! So start acting like you are a child of the King. Expect good things to happen.

The Challenge

Now you are ready
for...
THE CHALLENGE!

Friends,
consider yourself
officially
CHALLENGED
to
right *now*
right where you are
take what you have
and
do what you can
to change the world and save
the over four billion people who
are Lost without God!

Share of the Lord's goodness. Show the world his love through your love. Show them through your kindness. Show them through the smallest to the largest acts of kindness.

Be BOLD!

In other words,
be about your FATHER'S business!

Today is available to you!

Over the next few pages, we will explore some of the things you can do to change lives, to make a difference, so you can someday hear...

Well done thou good and faithful servant...
enter in.

What can I do for the Lord? You may say your funds are limited. Your health is not the best. You don't have the time. But there is something every one of us can do.

Next are some ideas to get you started. Friends, you can do this! Get started today. We challenge you!

If you have ZERO funds to work with you can:

- Contact a nursing home. Tell them, "I am interested in volunteering, I wonder if there is one person that comes to mind that doesn't get visitors that I could visit?" Then go visit them. Today! You don't have to have a thousand eloquent words to say, just sit with them. Let them talk. Sit with them some more. Things will come up that you can help with. Maybe help them eat their dinner. Maybe read the Bible to them. Maybe sing a song. Pray with them. Make sure everything is okay with them and the Lord. Be a friend!
- Church prayer lists. It doesn't cost anything to pray. Get your church prayer list. Get several churches' prayer lists. Lift the needs up to the Lord. He hears

and answers prayer. In James 5:16 (KJV), it says, "The effectual fervent prayer of a righteous man availeth much." There are many scriptures that encourage us to pray. Pray, be faithful to your prayer life.

- Cards. Get the sick list at churches. Or the birthday list, and send cards. Cards are so encouraging and thoughtful. You don't have to say anything but a simple greeting and put in a scripture that will encourage them.
- Can't afford stamps? Call your local church and let them know you would like to work in this ministry with cards of encouragement. Would they be able to help you mail them? In the same token, get folks at church to bring a box of cards or the cards they get in the mail from the veterans or other agencies.
- There are lots of free options. Don't stop at the first no, just say "I wonder if you could help me connect with someone in the church who would like to be a part of this encouraging ministry?" Maybe a note in the bulletin.

You will be planting seeds of hope. You can do this! Other ideas of free service:

- Can you bring your neighbors' trash can back from the road?
- Can you mow? Shovel snow? Rake leaves?
- Hugs. People need love!

- Can you share a plate of food with an elderly or sick neighbor? It does not have to be fancy. There are "to go" boxes at dollar stores or use a paper plate and foil. Share what you are having. Or share just a dessert to open the door of giving in this manner.
- Can you just step next door to say hello? "I'm Mary next door, just wanted to say hello and let you know where I live, and wondered if it would be okay to say hello now and again?" Offer your number if you like, offer "If you need me, I am just next door." Whatever you wish to offer, just be a friend.

If you have $100 or less per month to give to ministry:

- Food pantry. Go to your local food pantry and find out what the top few items needed in the pantry are. Maybe its spaghetti sauce. Go buy twenty-five jars of spaghetti sauce. Every month. Be faithful!
- Hygiene/snack. Take a gallon zip bag and fill it with items you would appreciate if you were homeless, like wipes, toothpaste, deodorant, can opener, McDonalds $5 gift card, hard candy, small Bible (mark some encouraging scriptures), daily devotional, peanut butter crackers, etc. Contact a police officer and get their recommendation on how to get them into the hands of the homeless. Or take them to soup kitchens and give them out outside to those who want one.

- Sponsor a child in need through agencies such as Save a Generation, World Vision, or Amazima.org. We have personally sponsored children through these agencies and know them to be legitimate in their desire to help feed, clothe, and educate children. Sponsorship is thirty to forty dollars per month. You can change a life!
- Provide the funds and/or order Christian literature for a local prison ministry.
- Find out if there is a prison chaplain and see what he/she needs.
- Contact your local electric, gas, or water company. Donate to keep someone's water or electricity on. Be specific. If you want to help someone with children or the elderly, just say so. Through our ministry, we have witnessed parents afraid their children would be taken from them due to their inability to provide water and electricity. You could really help a family with this need.
- Can't clean the church yourself? Volunteer the funds to pay for one week per month for the church to be cleaned by a cleaning service.
- Go to Family Dollar or Dollar General Stores. They have some pretty nice gift Bibles for $10. Highlight some of the scriptures of encouragement, then go to the hospital, ballgame, anywhere. Ask people, "Can I give you a gift? I highlighted some things to encourage you or make you smile."

- Help unemployed folks with their resume or complete an online application. Take them to their job interview.
- Gift cards from a grocery store. Take them to Social Services and get the supervisor to give them out as necessary to moms needing diapers.
- Gas cards. Buy some gas cards in small amounts and take them to the local unemployment office. Get them to give them to someone they feel is truly in need—like those who can't get a job because they lack the money for gas to get to work.

If you have over 100 dollars to give to God's Kingdom:

- Do all of the abovementioned areas of ministry, but in larger quantities.
- Donate to your local nonprofit. They see all of the urgent needs firsthand and generally have screening guidelines in place to assess the true need of a situation. No matter how big or how small your donation, it helps.
- Nursing home. Go to the administrator, see what you can buy for one of the residents. Some folks' entire check go to their care so there are no funds for their clothing, or underclothes, snack, gum, haircuts, etc. Most nursing and retirement homes have a stylist available for a minimal fee.

- Police officers generally have an item such as stuffed animals they like to give to children who are in crises situations. Check with your local police station and see if there is an area where you can be of service.
- Clean Water Missionary Resources has a list of charities who drill wells in underprivileged countries How rewarding is it to help provide clean, safe water to a village?
- Sponsor some teens for church mission trips. That's a win-win situation. You are planting seeds in a young life growing in Christ and you are helping the people assisted by the mission trip. *Twofold* opportunity to give! Yeah!
- Print some invitations to your church, get out in the community and invite people. Go, walk in boldness, sure you will get some "deer in the headlight" stares, but who cares? You are probably the only Jesus a lot of people will see. Smile and lovingly invite them to come to your church, and move on. No pressure. You planted the seed, God will do the rest.
- Get some Christian literature, Bibles, devotionals, etc., and a big bowl of candy. Everyone loves a piece of candy. Rent a day table at a flea/variety market. Smile, be a light for Jesus, and give your items away. You will be so glad you did.
- Watch for a shoe clearance at local stores. You can literally get shoes for five dollars or less in off-season sales. Collect them. When it is school time, go to the

public housing and set up a folding table and give out free shoes to the kids. Same could work for book bags, school supplies, coats, etc. When people try to thank us for this type thing, we always say, "A gift from God to you." To God be the glory.

Friends, the possibilities are endless. It doesn't matter how big or how small your work is for God. It all makes a difference. Sometimes you don't see the outcome of your seeds of goodness that you are sowing. But God does, and he has a record of them.

The Bible scripture that serves as the Mission Statement for our ministry is found in Matthew 25:40 (KJV). It reads:

> And the King shall answer and say unto them, Verily I say unto you, Inasmuch as ye have done it unto one of the least of these my brethren ye have done it unto Me.
>
> Then shall He also say to them on the left hand, Depart from Me, ye cursed, into everlasting fire, prepared for the devil and his angels:
>
> For I was an hungred, and ye gave me no meat: I was thirsty and ye gave me no drink:
>
> I was a stranger, and ye took me not in: naked, and ye clothed me not: sick, and in prison and ye visited me not.
>
> Then shall they also answer Him saying, Lord, when saw we Thee an hungred or athirst, or a stran-

ger, or naked, or sick, or in prison and did not minister unto Thee?

Then shall He answer them, saying, verily I say unto you, Inasmuch as ye did it not to one of the least of these, ye did it not to Me.

And these shall go away into everlasting punishment: but the righteous into life eternal.

Pretty eye-opening passage of scripture, isn't it? That should get us all working and striving to meet all the needs we possibly can. Do you get the impression from this passage that the Lord meant for us to do these things once in a while? Twice a year? No, it seems that every time these needs present themselves, we need to act.

Sometimes we let circumstance stand in our way of actually reaching out. It may be the idea of the people in the world who abuse generosity. Friends, when you have given something in good faith, it is now between them and God. You did your part. Certainly use wisdom and caution where needed, but after that, it is between them and God. There will be times you may have to help fifty to get to the five who urgently needed it. That's okay, do it anyway. The Bible says in Galatians 6:9, "And let us not grow weary in well doing: for in due season we shall reap if we faint not."

Have you ever "jumped in" on a task and amazed yourself how much you were able to accomplish in a very short time because of your focus and desire to finish? Our prayer is that you have a new desire to cross the "finish line" to the Lord with rewards a plenty! And that you have a new realization of the urgency to get started in your work for the Lord. We challenge you to have an entry for every day documenting what you did that day in honor of the Lord. Many days you will have several things to write. Wonderful! And some days you will have one thing to write. But do something every day! Will it be easy? Probably not, but do it anyway. Will you go to bed at night with peace in your heart that you did what was honorable and good? You bet!

Friends, it will be worth it all when you stand before the King of Kings and hear "well done, thou good and faithful servant!" God bless you as you begin this documentation of your daily ministry! You are going to amaze yourself!

Take the road less traveled

It will be an adventure!

DAY 1

Ecclesiastes 3:1–8

To everything there is a season, and a time to every purpose under the heaven: A time to be born, and a time to die; a time to plant, and a time to pluck up that which is planted; A time to kill, and a time to heal; a time to break down, and a time to build up; A time to weep, and a time to laugh; A time to mourn and a time to dance; A time to cast away stones, and a time to gather stones together; a time to embrace, and a time to refrain from embracing; A time to get, and a time to lose; a time to keep, and a time to cast away; A time to rend, and a time to sew, a time to keep silence, and a time to speak; A time to love, and a time to hate; a time of war, and a time of peace.

Idea for the Challenge

Today could be a day of making peace. The Bible says, "Blessed are the peacemakers for they shall be called the children of God." Although we may not always feel we were the ones in the wrong, it is pleasing to God for us to love each other enough to make peace. Is there someone you could make peace with today?

Something to Consider

1. Would I really lose anything by making peace?
2. What could I gain by making peace?
3. Who am I hurting when I hold a grudge?

Day 1 _____

Lord, today was a time of Peace…

_____

_____

_____

_____

_____

_____

_____

_____

_____

_____

_____

_____

_____

_____

_____

_____

_____

DAY 2

Proverbs 17:22

A merry heart doeth good like a medicine: but a broken spirit drieth the bones.

Idea for the Challenge

Have you ever had a song stuck in your mind? For today, how about intentionally getting your heart singing something "merry"? The song that comes to mind is in most hymnals, it says, "I've got the Joy, Joy, Joy, Joy down in my heart, where? Down in my heart, where? Down in my heart." Can't sing? Print off the words of a merry song and post them, share them, post a Youtube video of a merry song.

Plant seeds of happiness!

Something to Consider

1. What kind of music do I listen to?
2. Is it encouraging me and/or my family?

3. If my family were asked to sing a positive song, would they know the words to one?

Day 2 _____

Today, I choose to be Merry and I will spread joy by…

_____

_____

_____

_____

_____

_____

_____

_____

_____

_____

_____

_____

_____

_____

_____

_____

DAY 3

Psalm 91:1

He that dwelleth in the secret place of the most High shall abide under the shadow of the Almighty.

Idea for the Challenge

What a message this scripture holds. You could make this your theme for the day. Ask everyone you encounter, "Did you know that when you live for Jesus Psalm's 91 says you abide under the shadow of the Almighty?" What a place of comforting peace!

You will be an encouragement by sharing this reminder!

Something to Consider

1. Can you imagine the greatness of God and what being in his shadow would truly mean?
2. Is there peace in your relationship with God?

3. Would anything or anyone be worth sacrificing that peace with him?

Day 3 _____

What a privilege it is to abide in the shadow of God. I will share of his goodness by...

_____

_____

_____

_____

_____

_____

_____

_____

_____

_____

_____

_____

_____

_____

_____

_____

DAY 4

John 14:16

And I will pray the Father, and He shall give you another Comforter, that He may abide with you forever.

Idea for the Challenge

"Comforter" refers to the Holy Spirit that lives inside of us as Christians. Did you know he directs you, guides you? Spend a few minutes in silence today. Ask the Holy Spirit to guide your path of service today. He will lead you, give you ideas. Listen. What do you feel led to do today?

Something to Consider

1. Can you recall times the Holy Spirit has led you in the past? Often noted as "something told me," "mother's intuition," etc.

2. Did you know the Bible says the Holy Spirit will teach you all things and bring all things to your remembrance? (John 14:26)
3. Could you benefit from taking time in your daily life to "listen" in your heart and mind for the Holy Spirit's guidance?

Day 4 _____

The Lord sent me a comforter, the Holy Spirit. Holy Spirit, be with me as I go share of Jesus's love as I...

_____

_____

_____

_____

_____

_____

_____

_____

_____

_____

_____

_____

_____

_____

_____

_____

DAY 5

Hebrews 10:23–24

Let us hold fast the profession of our faith without wavering for he is faithful that promised
　　And let us consider one another to provoke unto love and to good works

Idea for the Challenge

A day to do good works. The possibilities are endless. Sow right where you are, use what you have, and do what you can do—for others, of course. Do you have too much of something? Give it away.

Something to Consider

1. When we consider one another as mentioned in this scripture, are we provoking people in our life to wrath or to good?

2. Do you know which "buttons" of your friends and family *not* to push?
3. How about we declare not to intentionally push buttons of wrath, deal?

Day 5 _____

Lord, I am holding fast to the faith. Today I will use all that you have given me to bless others by...

_____

_____

_____

_____

_____

_____

_____

_____

_____

_____

_____

_____

_____

_____

_____

_____

DAY 6

2 Timothy 1:7

For God hath not given us the spirit of fear; but of power, and of love, and of a sound mind.

Idea for the Challenge

Hmm...NO FEAR. This is a day to be fearless for our Lord. If we were not afraid, and fearless, I bet we would let our concern for our friend's and family's eternity make us bold enough to say, "I love you, and I just want to make sure we are going to spend eternity together. Have you asked Jesus into your heart? Would you like to? I will pray with you!" Christians are not perfect, just forgiven.

Something to Consider

1. What is your biggest fear about sharing the gift of salvation?

2. Is the fear of seeing your loved ones forever lost bigger than that fear?
3. What will you do about it?

Day 6 _____

I am not given to fear, but power, love, and a sound mind. I will boldly be about my Father's business by...

_____

_____

_____

_____

_____

_____

_____

_____

_____

_____

_____

_____

_____

_____

DAY 7

Romans 15:7

Wherefore receive ye one another, as Christ also received us to the glory of God.

Idea for the Challenge

What can you do today? Put the glory of God on grace, kindness, and humility. Make it a determination in your heart that every single person you meet today, you will "receive" them as you would imagine Christ receiving you. You are going to be so blessed, and be a blessing at the same time.

Something to Consider

1. How would you expect others to respond to your greeting them with such love?
2. Would you say that making this type of reception of people part of our daily lives will help eliminate any

issues we may have toward family/friends who have hurt us in the past?

3. When God receives us, is it with open arms? Are you holding back from him or greeting him with open arms?

Day 7 _____

Help me receive others as you, Lord, have received me. As I go into my day, my goal is to show others that I am yours by…

_____

_____

_____

_____

_____

_____

_____

_____

_____

_____

_____

_____

_____

_____

_____

_____

DAY 8

Matthew 10:16

Behold, I send you forth as sheep in the midst of
wolves: be ye therefore wise as serpents, and harmless as doves.

Idea for the Challenge

This scripture is a reminder that we should put on the
Armor of God described in Ephesians 6:11–24. Spend this
day sharing this important scripture with family, your children, your friends. Post it on social media, on your refrig-
erator etc. Meditate on this scripture and put it in your
heart. This scripture is so important!

Something to Consider

1. Why would we need the armor of God in our daily lives?
2. Would you consider yourself harmless as doves?

3. As you recall how God is ever present, will you begin to realize the importance of your every action?

Day 8 _____

Today, I ask for wisdom in all that I do, and I will be harmless as a dove as I...

_____

_____

_____

_____

_____

_____

_____

_____

_____

_____

_____

_____

_____

_____

_____

_____

DAY 9

Galatians 5:21

Envying's, Murders, drunkenness, revellings, and such like: of the which I tell you before as I have also told you in time past, that they which do such things shall not inherit the kingdom of God.

Idea for the Challenge

This would be a good day to share some copies of the Ten Commandments, located in Exodus 20. Print them off your computer, or stop by the Christian bookstore and get bookmarks with the commandments on them, and hand them out.

Something to Consider

1. Do you keep the commandments every day?
2. Did you know God said, "If you love me, keep my commandments" (John 14:15)?

Day 9 _____

A sin-free life is my goal. Help me share the things pleasing to you today, Lord, through…

_____

_____

_____

_____

_____

_____

_____

_____

_____

_____

_____

_____

_____

_____

_____

_____

_____

_____

DAY 10

Mark 16:15

Go ye into all the world, and preach the gospel to every creature.

Idea for the Challenge

You could choose to share God's word with someone not able to go to church by reading the Bible to them or share copies of your favorite recorded message from your church. Also, you could make a donation to a minister that you enjoy to help him or her continue in the ministry.

Something to Consider

1. When was the first time you heard the Gospel of Christ?
2. Who in your life is a Christian example?
3. Whose eyes are on *you* as a Christian example? Are you doing all you can do to be a good example?
4. How can you improve?

Day 10 _____

Help me, Lord, as I proclaim your gospel. Today, I will boldly confess your word by...

_____

_____

_____

_____

_____

_____

_____

_____

_____

_____

_____

_____

_____

_____

_____

_____

DAY 11

Ephesians 4:29

Let no corrupt communication proceed out of your mouth, but that which is good to the use of edifying, that it may minister grace unto the hearers.

Idea for the Challenge

With *every* person you encounter today, speak kindly, uplifting, encouraging. Make a conscious decision to react with grace no matter what. Document the moments from today when you would have normally reacted differently but you were able to overcome and exhibited a gracious response. You were ministering as you were showing grace. Pretty neat, huh?

Something to Consider

1. Every thought and opinion does not need to come out of our mouth, agreed?

2. Will the faces of our friends, spouse, and children reflect and react in kind to our grace, or will their faces reflect and react to unkindness?

3. Have you thought about the potential impact your every word can have on others?

Day 11 _____

Today, I am declaring that every word from my mouth will be good. I pray everyone I speak to today will be encouraged. I...

_____

_____

_____

_____

_____

_____

_____

_____

_____

_____

_____

_____

_____

_____

_____

DAY 12

Isaiah 61:1

The Spirit of the Lord God is upon me; because the Lord hath anointed me to preach good tidings unto the meek; he hath sent me to bind up the broken-hearted to proclaim liberty to the captives, and the opening of the prison to them that are bound.

Idea for the Challenge

There are several types of imprisonment, but let's focus on actual prisoners behind bars.

What are the guidelines of your local prison about giving Bibles, hygiene, or snack items? You could plan a visit with a group through the prison chaplain or possibly the chaplain has items he needs to help those imprisoned. You can indeed encourage and give hope to the hopeless. You can change the world through your goodness.

Something to Consider

1. Imagine what it must be like to be in prison—no one around who cares about you, no hugs, tick-tock goes the clock, pretty much hopeless, wouldn't you imagine?
2. Wouldn't you imagine even the smallest acts of kindness would speak volumes?
3. What would you want someone to do if you were in that situation?

Day 12 _____

I ask you, Lord, to anoint me anew. Today I will share your good tidings by...

_____

_____

_____

_____

_____

_____

_____

_____

_____

_____

_____

_____

_____

_____

_____

_____

DAY 13

Ephesians 4:26

Let not the sun go down on your wrath.

Idea for the Challenge

Make amends where you need to make amends. Haven't done anything big but feel like you didn't deal with someone as good as you should have? Right the wrong. If that is not possible, do a good deed/gesture toward that person(s).

Something to Consider

1. Wouldn't you agree that the longer you are angry with someone, the bigger the problem becomes?
2. The easy road is to get mad, but what could you do instead?
3. What can you do to promote peace in your home? At work?

Day 13 _____

Today I will examine my heart. Am I angry with anyone? I will make amends by...

_____

_____

_____

_____

_____

_____

_____

_____

_____

_____

_____

_____

_____

_____

_____

_____

DAY 14

James 4:6–7

God resisteth the proud but giveth grace unto the humble.

Submit yourselves therefore to God. Resist the devil, and he will flee from you.

Idea for the Challenge

It doesn't take long in our daily routine until we come across people in person or on the phone who have something wrong with them or something wrong in their lives. Let this be your scripture to share today. At the name of Jesus the devil has to flee, stand on it, and declare it with confidence! Amen? Amen!

Something to Consider

1. First Peter 5:8 says the devil is seeking whom he may devour.

2. When things come against you, do you command the devil to leave?

3. Do we pat the devil on the back and go ahead with our negative talk about the situation? Do you think he loves that affirmation?

Day 14 _____

Lord, I approach this day you have given me with a humble heart. At the name of Jesus, the devil has to flee, so I will...

_____

_____

_____

_____

_____

_____

_____

_____

_____

_____

_____

_____

_____

_____

_____

_____

DAY 15

Romans 12:17

Provide things honest in the sight of all men

Idea for the Challenge

With your family, wife, husband, kids, etc., explore all the times you can be a "little" dishonest. Explore all the scriptures pertaining to dishonesty and make a written declaration to hold each other accountable for dishonesty, big or small. Examples of small things include taking a stack of napkins from a restaurant for your car. Ordering two samples on the internet with different names. Making the teacher think you left your homework at home when in reality you forgot to do the assignment.

Something to Consider

1. "If you love me, keep my commandments," Jesus says. Do you love him?

2. Are you showing him?
3. Are you creating an unshakable foundation of faith for your family, friends, and children to rely on?

Day 15 _____

Today I will make a point of being 100% honest in all that I do.

    I can…

_____

_____

_____

_____

_____

_____

_____

_____

_____

_____

_____

_____

_____

_____

_____

_____

DAY 16

1 Timothy 6:19

Laying up in store for themselves a good foundation against the time to come, that they may lay hold on eternal life.

Idea for the Challenge

The things you spend your money on in this life are of no use to you in eternity. But the things that you invest in for the Gospel's sake are eternal. Find the things that will change lives, help ministries, etc. Declare today a new way you can invest in your eternity and do it, today!

Something to Consider

1. How much do you think you have spent for God this past year?
2. How much do you think you have spent on other things?

3. Did you know Jesus told a rich man in the Bible to sell all he had, give it to the poor, and follow him? (Luke 18:22)

Day 16 _____

My focus today is laying up treasure in heaven so that I may lay hold on eternal life. I can invest in my eternal life by...

_____

_____

_____

_____

_____

_____

_____

_____

_____

_____

_____

_____

_____

_____

_____

_____

DAY 17

Colossians 3:16–17

Let the word of Christ dwell in you richly in all wisdom; teaching and admonishing one another in psalms and hymns and spiritual songs, singing with grace in your hearts to the Lord.

And whatsoever ye do in word or deed, do all in the name of the Lord Jesus, giving thanks to God and the Father by him.

Idea for the Challenge

Post an uplifting Christian Song on social media. Buy or share Christian music CDs, with a note "To encourage you" and the above scripture reference.

Something to Consider

1. Did you notice that the above scripture says whatever you do in word or deed, do it in the name of the Lord Jesus?
2. Are there words in your daily vocabulary that wouldn't be honorable?
3. Would your deeds confirm or dispel that you are a Christian?

Day 17 _____

Today, I will praise you, Lord, with Song and give thanks to God. I will...

_____

_____

_____

_____

_____

_____

_____

_____

_____

_____

_____

_____

_____

_____

_____

_____

DAY 18

1 John 2:4–6

He that saith, I know him, and keepeth not his commandments, is a liar, and the truth is not in him.

But whoso keepeth his word, in him verily is the love of God perfected: hereby know we that we are in him.

He that saith he abideth in him ought himself also so to walk, even as he walked.

Idea for the Challenge

Give someone the gift of God's word. Dollar general/family dollar/Walmart have gift Bibles for around $10, or print some uplifting scriptures from your computer, or hand write encouraging scriptures on index cards that you put in a zip lock with a note of "I wrote these to encourage you."

Something to Consider

1. Examine your daily walk, are you keeping his commandments every day, all day?
2. What change would make your walk more like his walk, as mentioned in verse 6?
3. Did you absorb that if you keep his word, the love of God is perfected in you? Pretty awesome hug from God, isn't it?

Day 18 _____

We will keep your word so that the love of God can be perfected. I will...

_____

_____

_____

_____

_____

_____

_____

_____

_____

_____

_____

_____

_____

_____

_____

_____

DAY 19

Philippians 1:3

I thank my God upon every remembrance of you

Idea for the Challenge

Take blank greeting cards and write this scripture and send to the people in your life who mean a lot to you.

Something to Consider

1. Are you remembering friends and family with thankful hearts?
2. Are you focused on the positive that people bring into your life, or the negative?
3. Bring to mind the one person who troubles you the most, decide on at least one factor you can be thankful for about them. Let that be the positive that comes to mind next time you remember them.

Day 19 _____

Thanking God for you! I will...

_____

_____

_____

_____

_____

_____

_____

_____

_____

_____

_____

_____

_____

_____

_____

_____

_____

_____

DAY 20

1 John 3:1

Behold, what manner of love the Father hath bestowed upon us, that we should be called the sons of God.

Idea for the Challenge

Think of all the children in orphanages who feel they have no parent. Put together a treat basket or a few treats tied up in a bow in tissue paper. Put today's scripture on a card with "Sending big hugs your way. God bless you."

Something to Consider

1. Do you have good parents? Bad parents? Do you have no parents?
2. Do you carry little or big hurts because of something they did or didn't do?

3. Give all hurts to God, leave the past in the past, God is still working on all of us! Step forward in forgiveness and in the truth that we are called "the sons of God."

Day 20 _____

I am a child of God. I am loved, so today I am going to show his love to others by...

_____

_____

_____

_____

_____

_____

_____

_____

_____

_____

_____

_____

_____

_____

_____

_____

DAY 21

Job 2:13

So they sat down with him upon the ground seven days and seven nights, and none spake a word unto him: for they saw his grief was very great.

Idea for the Challenge

Stop in the nursing home and choose to sit with the person in the worst health. Pray for them.

Words are not needed. Your presence and friendship is!

Something to Consider

1. Faithful friends! Would you stay with a friend seven days if needed?
2. Do your friends know you are a faithful friend?
3. What could you do to develop the unshakeable type of friendship?

Day 21 _____

Words are not always needed. My silent friendship can bring comfort. Today, I will…

_____

_____

_____

_____

_____

_____

_____

_____

_____

_____

_____

_____

_____

_____

_____

_____

_____

_____

DAY 22

Psalm 136:1

O Give thanks unto the Lord; for He is good: for His mercy endureth forever

Idea for the Challenge

Tell of your thanks unto the Lord all day in every way. Text it, Facebook it, write it on your rear window, put a sign in your yard. Thank you, God, for all of your blessings on me!

Something to Consider

1. What are the top five things you are thankful for?
2. What are you least thankful for?
3. In your prayer time, are you mostly giving thanks or requests?

Day 22 _____

Heavenly Father, I give thanks unto you. You are worthy to
be praised! I will...

_____

_____

_____

_____

_____

_____

_____

_____

_____

_____

_____

_____

_____

_____

_____

_____

DAY 23

1 Peter 3:12

For the eyes of the Lord are over the righteous, and his ears are open unto their prayers

Idea for the Challenge

Make this a day of prayer for others. Pray for our nation, our soldiers, our leaders, our ministers. Pray for everyone! Spend extra time knelt in prayer.

Something to Consider

1. Did you notice that God's ears are open to our prayers, not closed?
2. Do you think he wants to hear from you, his child, regularly?
3. Did you know that the Bible says to "pray without ceasing" (1 Thessalonians 5:17)? Talk to him, he is your best friend, your Father. He loves you unconditionally.

Day 23 _____

Thank you, Lord, for hearing my prayers. I will pray for…

_____

_____

_____

_____

_____

_____

_____

_____

_____

_____

_____

_____

_____

_____

_____

_____

_____

_____

DAY 24

Matthew 24:42

Watch therefore: for ye know not what hour your Lord doth come.

Idea for the Challenge

Spend a few minutes jotting down things you would do if you knew the Lord was coming today. Then do at least one of them.

Something to Consider

1. Are you watching for the Lord?
2. Are you living your life like *this* could be the day of his return?
3. Is *this* the day you step into eternity?
4. What would you like to change in your life if you knew this was the day you are appointed to stand before him?

Day 24 _____

Father, you may come today! So I will...

_____

_____

_____

_____

_____

_____

_____

_____

_____

_____

_____

_____

_____

_____

_____

_____

_____

DAY 25

Matthew 5:16

Let your light so shine before men that they may
see your good works, and glorify your Father which
is in heaven.

Idea for the Challenge

Volunteer before work, during lunch, after work, for at least
thirty minutes at a charity, animal shelter, nursing home,
etc. Humbly in and humbly out. Let your light shine.

Something to Consider

1. When you do good works, do you expect a pat on the
   back?
2. Do you do good works so that your Heavenly Father
   will be glorified?
3. Let's make a decision to set our minds on bringing
   glory to God, leaving self behind.

Day 25 _____

I am letting my light shine before men to bring you honor,
Lord. I will...

_____

_____

_____

_____

_____

_____

_____

_____

_____

_____

_____

_____

_____

_____

_____

_____

DAY 26

Psalm 139:14

I will praise thee; I am fearfully and wonderfully made: marvelous are thy works: and that my soul knoweth right well.

Idea for the Challenge

Today is focused on you. Let the knowledge of your being wonderfully made sink into your inner being. Do not say *one* negative thing about yourself. You are God's masterpiece. Share with someone else that they are wonderfully made by God.

Something to Consider

1. Since you are God's masterpiece, let's praise him for wonderfully making you.
2. Did you know God inhabits the praises of his people?

3. Envision two baskets in your life, one is your prayer basket and one is your praise basket. Are both baskets equally full?

Day 26 _____

I am wonderfully made! I will...

_____

_____

_____

_____

_____

_____

_____

_____

_____

_____

_____

_____

_____

_____

_____

_____

DAY 27

John 15:13

Greater love hath no man than this, that a man lay down his life for his friends.

Idea for the Challenge

Lay down one of your favorite things today and use the money or time for someone else. Give up cigarettes, Starbucks, fast food, etc. today. Use the four dollars you saved on blessing someone else. For example, get a rose for a widow. Get a couple of snacks for the homeless man on the corner. If you are laying down your favorite TV show, that time could be used encouraging someone else. Lay it down.

Something to Consider

1. Could you lay down your life for friends?

2. Did you realize Jesus could have stopped his crucifixion, but continued being tortured for you and for me?
3. Why did he lay down his life? (1 Corinthians 15:3)

Day 27 _____

You laid down your life for me, Lord. I will…

_____

_____

_____

_____

_____

_____

_____

_____

_____

_____

_____

_____

_____

_____

_____

_____

DAY 28

Acts 2:44

And all that believed were together, and had all things common

Idea for the Challenge

Today, let's have breakfast, lunch, or dinner with some of our believing friends. We can lift each other up and be a source of encouragement. And enjoy the peace of being with brothers and sisters in Christ.

Something to Consider

1. Did you know the Bible says not to fail to assemble ourselves together? (Hebrews 10:25)
2. Why would we benefit from being together with other Christians?
3. Should we judge our brothers and sisters? (Romans 14:10–13)

Day 28 _____

Thank you, Lord, for my friends who believe in you. I will…

_____

_____

_____

_____

_____

_____

_____

_____

_____

_____

_____

_____

_____

_____

_____

_____

_____

_____

DAY 29

2 Peter 3:18

But grow in grace, and in the knowledge of our Lord and Savior Jesus Christ. To him be glory both now and forever Amen

Idea for the Challenge

Focus on growing in knowledge of our Lord. Write down a short list of fun Bible facts and share them with others today. For example, the top ten miracles of the Bible.

Something to Consider

1. Are you operating in grace?
2. What are some traits of someone you consider graceful/gracious?
3. Did you know that it is by grace through faith that you are saved? (Ephesians 2:8–9)

Day 29 _____

I want to grow in the grace and knowledge of you, Lord.
Today, I will…

_____

_____

_____

_____

_____

_____

_____

_____

_____

_____

_____

_____

_____

_____

_____

_____

_____

DAY 30

Galatians 6:10

As we have therefore opportunity, let us do good unto all men, especially unto them who are of the household of faith.

Idea for the Challenge

You could take this opportunity to do something special for your pastor and his wife, Sunday school teachers, or others. Possibly a gift card for a nice dinner, or a card of thanks for their faithful service.

Something to Consider

1. Read today's scripture reference again. How would you respond to these questions below?
2. Could I borrow your mower? Mine is broken.
3. Could you give me a ride to work?
4. I can't find my dog, have you seen it?

5. What is your initial response? Be honest.
6. What should your response be? (Galatians 6:10)

Day 30 _____

Thank you, Lord, for helping me recognize all the opportunities today to do good to all men. I will do good to others by...

_____

_____

_____

_____

_____

_____

_____

_____

_____

_____

_____

_____

_____

_____

_____

_____

_____

_____

Congratulations, you have completed the thirty-day challenge!

Take a few minutes to reflect individually or as a group:

- Have you grown these past thirty days?
- Were you challenged to do more than you normally would have done?
- Were you forced to step outside your comfort zone?
- Recall the people you helped. How many lives do you think you touched by taking the challenge?
- What was the best thing that happened?

Pretty amazing, isn't it?

Keep serving the Lord! Each and every day!

You are changing other's lives, and your eternity!

God bless you!

Feel free to share your success with us, we love to hear how God is working. Our e-mail address is TheFathersStore@aol.com. Mailing address is P.O. Box 2371 Thomasville, NC 27361.

To invite the Wards to come share with your church on serving God through serving others, please e-mail them at TheFathersStore@aol.com.

Contact information for charitable organizations mentioned in this book:

- Save a Generation
  P.O. Box 370 Carolina Beach, NC
  28428

- World Vision
  P.O. Box 9716 Federal Way, WA
  98063

- Amazima.org
- www.MissionaryResources.com